MONEY DOES MATTER

AND SO DOES HOW YOU HANDLE IT!

MONEY DOES MATTER
AND SO DOES HOW YOU HANDLE IT!

CHANDRA L. WINFORD

P.O. Box 742978 • Riverdale, Georgia 30274
Email: cwinfordfinancial@gmail.com
www.moneymattercw.com

CONTENTS

SECTION I:
IS PROSPERITY FOR ME ?

SECTION II:
WHAT IS MY PROSPERITY PLAN?

SECTION III:
HOW CAN I PROTECT MY PROSPERITY?

ACKNOWLEDGEMENT

I would like to acknowledge my husband, Willie for being a support and allowing me to take the time to focus on revising and finishing this book.

Also, I want to thank Bishop Kenneth Fuller for coming up with the title during a brainstorming session for a workshop that I was doing. Immediately when he spoke the title, I knew that was it!

Foreword

Are you wondering how to get your finances in order, but you aren't sure where to start? Money (or a lack of it) is one of those areas that continues to frustrate people as they live paycheck to paycheck, many times barely able to make ends meet. The truth is that it is not God's will for anyone to be in debt and live in lack and insufficiency. However, there is a practical side to money management that a lot of people don't understand. Chandra Winford's insightful book *Money Does Matter and So Does How You Handle It!* shows you how to get your finances in order so that you can truly live the abundant life God has designed for you.

This book answers some of the key questions that so many Christians ask pertaining to the financial aspect of prosperity. Things like, *Is prosperity for me?* and *How do I plan for and secure my financial future?* As a financial consultant, Chandra has experience advising clients of all backgrounds and walks of life, and she has also seen the power of God move in her own finances as she walked out the process of debt cancellation. Her experiences and knowledge about money management have proven to be invaluable and have given her the tools she needs to help others reach their financial potential.

Money Does Matter and So Does How You Handle It! not only provides a strong spiritual foundation of biblical understanding about money matters, it also provides wisdom tips on a practical level that are easy for anyone to understand and apply. The worksheets, expense tracker, and monthly spending plan, as well as the debt-elimination strategies, will put you on the right track and help you achieve your financial goals.

Financial empowerment is God's will for us, and He has given us the resources we need to live an abundant life on this Earth. *Money Does Matter and So Does How You Handle It!* shows you how to add corresponding action to your faith for maximum results.

Creflo Dollar
Senior Pastor and CEO
World Changers Church International

"Faithful is He Who is calling you [to Himself] and utterly trustworthy, and He will also do it [fulfill His call by hallowing and keeping you],"

1 THESSALONIANS 5:24, *THE AMPLIFIED BIBLE*

INTRODUCTION

THE FINANCIAL TEST

Let's face it – money, in all aspects, is a very touchy subject for most people. Whether extremely wealthy or barely making ends meet, people have a tendency to shy away from money matters. Even worse, very few people actually understand how to effectively manage and budget their finances. *I know because I have been there!*

As a financial consultant, when I sit down with my clients, most people wonder what qualifies me to speak to them about their finances. I'd like to credit my wisdom in the area of finances strictly to my education, but the reality is I've had to overcome some financial situations and challenges myself. It's through those life lessons that I am able to write this book with confidence. So let's begin by walking through my journey; which began on April 27, 2003.

At that time, I was up to my neck in debt. With more than $50,000 in credit card debt hanging over my head, I decided it was time to examine my financial situation and myself.

During this examination process I had to be real with myself. If I wanted to make a change and become debt free, I had to get to the root of the problem; which would require brutal honesty.

1. **I am a Christian, and while I do believe in tithing 10%** of all my income to the Lord, I'd not been totally consistent in this area. I did tithe the majority of the time, but if I believed God was my source I needed to be consistent in honoring Him with my tithe.

   "Every man according as he purposeth in his heart, so let him give; not grudgingly, or of necessity: for God loveth a cheerful giver," - 2 CORINTHIANS 9:7

2. **I had a fear of lack—a fear of not having enough to meet my needs.** This started from my childhood. I grew up in a home where it was hard for my parents to pay all the bills, so we had to make sacrifices; however, the Word says God has not given me the spirit of fear, but a spirit of love and a sound mind. I needed to begin confessing my faith in this area to help me overcome this fear and to build my confidence in God's Word concerning Him taking care of me financially.

   "For God hath not given us the spirit of fear; but of power, and of love, and of a sound mind," - 2 TIMOTHY 1:7

3. **I was an impulsive shopper at times.** When I had a strong desire to get something, I would use credit or go into debt to obtain it. I knew that I needed to change in this area. I found that if I left the item I desired at the store and went home and thought about it a little more before making the purchase, I usually found I could do without the items I thought I so desperately needed.

   "But my God shall supply all your need according to his riches in glory by Christ Jesus," - PHILIPPIANS 4:19

4. **I have always been a person who did budgets and planning** to ensure household items were paid first. This was a habit I needed to continue. It allowed me to set limits on what was really available for entertainment and personal purchases.

   "He becometh poor that dealeth with a slack hand: but the hand of the diligent maketh rich," - PROVERBS 10:4

5. **I had been married for a couple of years** and my husband's spending patterns were opposite of mine. He would just spend before considering household items; however we needed to work as a couple to ensure both our incomes were used to first pay household items before spending on other items.

   "Submitting yourselves one to another in the fear of God," - EPHESIANS 5:21

6. **I did not save. My savings were minimal.** I knew from my financial background that you should save at least two to three months of your salary for emergencies, but it seemed like I would always find a way to end up spending what little I would save.

MY FINANCES WERE OUT OF CONTROL! Everyone wanted to get paid, but my finances were tight! I began to pray and seek counsel from God to assist me in getting out of debt. On November 25, 2003, God reminded me that I was a financial teacher to the Body of Christ, and He wanted me to be restored so I could assist others in their restoration process. He gave me the following scriptures of restoration.

   "Call unto me, and I will answer thee, and show thee great and mighty things, which thou knowest not," - JEREMIAH 33:3

   "And it shall be to me a name of joy, a praise and an honour before all the nations of the earth, which shall hear all the good that I do unto them: and they shall fear and tremble for all the goodness and for all the prosperity that I procure unto It," - JEREMIAH 33:9

Three years prior in 2000, the Lord allowed me to start writing this book about prosperity. So I asked myself how I had arrived at this place. I was supposed to be the one helping others succeed, but when I looked around, the people I had counseled were exceeding me financially.

Today, I have learned that my anointing is not just for me, but for others. My anointing will be strongest if my love and purpose for debt freedom and debt release is to assist others.

Here are some of the things I had to experience and overcome to be able to finish this book and become qualified to teach on restoration of credit and finances:

- ✓ Creditors threatening to garnish my wages
- ✓ Creditors calling two to three times a day harassing me over the phone
- ✓ Feeling like I was a bad person because I did not have the funds to pay my bills
- ✓ Using credit cards to pay for my day-to-day needs
- ✓ Losing my job due to downsizing
- ✓ Foreclosure of my home
- ✓ Receiving bad treatment when trying to purchase a car, a house, furniture, etc.

Through the precious blood of Jesus, I was empowered to go through each of these trials and come out without the smell of smoke, just like the three Hebrew boys in the book of Daniel (Daniel 3:26). Now, the Lord has released me to publish this book.

"And the LORD appointed a set time, saying,

To morrow the LORD shall do this thing in the land,"

EXODUS 9:5

SECTION I

IS PROSPERITY FOR ME?

APPOINTED TIME FOR DEBT FREEDOM

Now is the appointed time God has set to financially prosper His people. We are at a point in the world's financial economy where their systems are failing.

The Lord has anointed me to teach financial prosperity for this appointed time and He is commanding the release of His people from financial bondage. We have been held in financial bondage for hundreds of years. In a similar manner, as the Lord brought the Israelites out of Egypt with jewels of silver and gold (Exodus11:2), God wants to show Himself strong on our behalf.

God is looking to use people who are willing vessels and who are faithful and obedient to His commandments (written Word and spoken voice) (2 Chronicles16:9). God gave us dominion and authority when He created man, but Adam lost that dominion and authority when he sinned in the Garden of Eden. Jesus restored that dominion back to us when God raised Him from the dead.

This plan of God is awesome because the Gentiles, those that are not saved, shall leave their inheritance to the righteous, and all will see thy glory and honor (Isaiah 62:2). It is going to require great faithfulness, the love of God, confession, and perseverance.

Romans 13:8 reads, *"Owe no man anything, but to love one another."* God wants us to owe no man and be free to love without any attachments. You are not totally free if you do not have the finances to complete the mission God has given to you.

It is the responsibility of the Church, both you and I, to go into the land and minister the Word of God. Into the land means in your own community as well as other communities. This requires financial resources, but God cannot put the money into your hand until you show yourself faithful with what He has already entrusted to you (Matthew 25:21). You have to get out of debt on purpose and renew your mind with Scriptures concerning your finances (Ephesians 4:23). If your mind is not renewed, debt-freedom will not be accomplished.

Let's begin the process of learning how to remove our debts. It is going to require sacrifice, discipline, and prayer. It means turning from your old way of doing things to God's way of doing things. Prayer will be essential! You will definitely need the Holy Spirit to help strengthen and guide you through this process.

FOUNDATIONS OF PROSPERITY

There are certain foundations we must possess in order to prosper in God's Kingdom. I have learned to take my financial intensity up a level since taking a Biblical Prosperity class. There are some keys that we must learn to ensure our foundation is firm. The keys are as follows:

- ✓ Knowing Your Covenant Rights
- ✓ Learning to Live as the Righteousness of God
- ✓ Having Faith in God's Word Concerning Finances
- ✓ Putting Your Faith Into Action

Many Christians have read or heard that God wants to prosper His people, but few have experienced manifestations of it in their lives. Let's examine each of these keys so we can be in position to experience God's promise of financial prosperity.

Knowing Your Covenant Rights

Covenant is a strong word. It is a sacred agreement between two or more people to agree to do or not to do something. God made a covenant with Abraham. He later allowed us to partake of that covenant through the death and resurrection of Jesus Christ. If you are an heir and you have a right to your parent's possession when they pass, you can only receive it if you are aware of it and follow the procedures necessary to receive the inheritance. God has left us an inheritance of riches and blessings, but we are not following the procedures to take possession of God's promises in our lives. On page 24, I show you your covenant rights based upon the Word of God. God responds to His Word and covenant, not to our emotions.

Learning to Live as the Righteousness of God

"But seek ye first the kingdom of God, and his righteousness;
and all these things shall be added unto you,"
MATTHEW 6:33

The righteousness of God is being in right standing with God. It's not something you can earn by doing works. It is a gift given by God when you get born-again. All you have to do is believe and receive that you have been made righteous.

"Even the righteousness of God which is by faith of Jesus Christ
unto all and upon all them that believe: for there is no difference,"
ROMANS 3:22

How do you live in right standing with God?

You learn what righteous people do by reading and mediating on God's Word. You continue in your righteous by obeying the Word of GOD in every area of your life. Receiving the Holy Spirit is essential because it is His assignment to lead and guide us into all righteousness.

"But the Comforter, which is the Holy Ghost, whom the Father will
send in my name, he shall teach you all things, and bring all things
to your remembrance, whatsoever I have said unto you,"
JOHN 14:26

Having Faith in God's Word Concerning Finances

Faith comes by hearing, and hearing the Word of God. If you are not hearing the Word of God concerning your finances, you are not developing faith in this area. You have to search the Bible to find scriptures that speak about God's purpose for your finances. I will share some of them with you now. Begin to meditate and study these scriptures.

"If they obey and serve him, they shall spend their days in prosperity, and their years in pleasures," - JOB 36:11

"For promotion cometh neither from the east, nor from the west, nor from the south. But God is the judge: he putteth down one, and setteth up another," - PSALM 75:6, 7

"But thou shalt remember the LORD thy God: for it is he that giveth thee power to get wealth, that he may establish his covenant which he sware unto thy fathers, as it is this day," - DEUTERONOMY 8:18

"O LORD, how manifold are thy works! in wisdom hast thou made them all: the earth is full of thy riches," - PSALM 104:24

"Praise ye the LORD. Blessed is the man that feareth the LORD, that delighteth greatly in his commandments. His seed shall be mighty upon earth: the generation of the upright shall be blessed. Wealth and riches shall be in his house: and his righteousness endureth for ever," - PSALM 112:1-3

"Wealth gotten by vanity shall be diminished: but he that gathereth by labour shall increase," - PROVERBS 13:11

"A good man leaveth an inheritance to his children's children: and the wealth of the sinner is laid up for the just," - PROVERBS 13:22

Begin by studying these scriptures. Then start making daily confessions two to three times a day concerning your finances. Take these scriptures and make them personal to you and your household. Reread and meditate on them until you see the results.

Satan will try to get you to believe this will not work for you, but I am a living witness that if you press through every financial trial confessing what God's Word says instead of your current circumstance, things will change.

Putting Your Faith Into Action

Putting your faith into action means doing the Word of God! It is more than just hearing the Word of God. It also means that you are not only confessing God's Word on finances, but you are doing what His Word says. The key is you have to begin to do it where you are right now. Do not wait for things to change. You have to show yourself faithful with the little before God will make you ruler over much.

If you are not giving 10% of your income to God let this be your starting point. You should also begin to pray each time you get a paycheck. Ask God how do you want me to use these funds? Also, ask for direction about who you can bless and be quick to obey once God gives you directions. Your faith will increase as you see the manifestation of God's Word.

Also, get a journal to write down your confessions and the victories as God brings them to pass. This journal can also be used as a reminder to you of what has been accomplished through your faith in God's Word.

I can recall a time when God told me to give a lady at church $25. When I approached the lady and told her what God told me she began crying. She told me she prayed to God and said, if this is the church you will have me to join send me a sign. She also stated that $25 was the exact amount she had put in the offering. She said she knew right then that this was her church and thanked me for obeying Him. It made me feel so good to be used by God to help someone else.

There were many times when people needed food or bills paid and because I obeyed God, I was able to be a blessing to them.

FINANCIAL PROSPERITY CONFESSION

The Lord is my shepherd; **I shall not want** any good thing promised according to His Word.

God orders my steps to follow His path into my **destiny of financial prosperity**.

The fear of the Lord causes me to have **no wants**!

I am obedient to the Word of God and **I am quick to obey**.

All of my needs are met, I am out of debt and I am blessed to be a blessing.

The Lord teaches me to profit through His holy Word, and I walk in faith and not by sight. It does not matter what it looks, feels, or sounds like; **I believe and trust the Word of God**.

God will supply **all my needs** according to His riches in glory.

I am submitted to God's will concerning my finances.

Enemies may come, but they shall not prosper against me because **the Lord is my buckler and shield**.

Scripture references:
Psalms 18:30, 23, 27:5, 27:10, 33:20, 119:133; Isaiah 5:17, 48:17; 2 Corinthians 5:7

PRAYER FOR BREAKING GENERATIONAL FINANCIAL BONDAGE

Right now I'm speaking to anyone who was raised in a family where there was shortage or lack. It can also apply to anyone who can recall seeing members of your family struggle to make ends meet. That is a generational curse. I want you to stop right now and repeat after me.

Heavenly Father, I thank you that You created me in Your image. You loved me and died for me before I was created in my mother's womb. Your Son, Jesus, died on the cross for me that I may have life, and have it more abundantly. You sent Your Son Jesus to pay the price for me. He took stripes on His back for my sin and iniquity.

Therefore, I break, pull up and cast away from me every generational curse of financial bondage at the root. I receive my inheritance of freedom from financial bondage and shortage. I refuse to live from paycheck to paycheck or robbing from Peter to pay Paul.

I make a quality decision to live debt free. I make a quality decision to operate in overflow and in increase. I have a covenant right to be free from debt and lack. The Lord will teach me how to profit and show me how to walk in line with His promises concerning my finances.

Lord, I acknowledge that my spirit man is perfect and complete. Father, I draw out the wisdom within my spirit concerning freedom from debt and I thank You Lord that You will assist me in renewing my mind in how I handle my finances. You also said in Your Word that You would honor those who honor You. I start by honoring You with my financial seed. I commit to sow into Your kingdom ten percent of all that You allow to flow through my hands.

Lord, You will give me witty inventions and the wisdom of how to put the plan into action.

Scripture references:
Genesis 1:27; Romans 5:8; John 10:10; Psalms 85:2, 89:34; Deuteronomy 8:18

IMPORTANCE OF OBEDIENCE

We tie God's hand from blessing us with things He has laid up for us when we are in disobedience. Delayed or partial obedience is still considered disobedience. Total obedience means doing exactly what God says. No exceptions!

God desires and wants us to have our stuff! We must learn to obey His Word and voice so He can trust us to do His will and not our own.

> *"For My thoughts are not your thoughts, neither are your ways my ways, saith the Lord. For as the heavens are higher than the earth, so are my ways higher than your ways, and my thoughts than your thoughts,"* - ISAIAH 55:8, 9

> *"Casting down imaginations, and every high thing that exalteth itself against the knowledge of God, and bringing into captivity every thought to the obedience of Christ,"* - 2 CORINTHIANS 10:5

Obedience to God sometimes means not doing some things you want to do in order to fulfill God's purpose for your life.

CONFESSIONS

It is vital for you to begin to make daily confessions according to God's Word in order for you to build your faith, dispatch the angels, and obligate Jesus to bring your Words to pass.

Jesus is the High Priest over your confession (Hebrews 3:1)

Angels hearken unto the voice of the Word of God (Psalms 103:20)

Meditation of the Word of God will make you prosperous (Joshua 1:8)

Confession with your mouth and believing you receive builds your faith (John 17:20)

MEDITATION SCRIPTURES

God's Instructions

"Till I come, give attendance to reading, to exhortation, to doctrine. Neglect not the gift that is in thee which was given thee by prophecy, with the laying on of the hands of the presbytery. Meditate upon these things; give thyself wholly unto them; that thy profiting may appear to all," - 1 TIMOTHY 4:13-15

** God gives you explicit instructions on what you need to do in order for all, to see your profiting.

Bondage

"The rich ruleth over the poor, and the borrower is servant to the lender," - PROVERBS 22:7

"Owe no man anything, but to love one another," - ROMANS 13:8

"My people are destroyed for lack of knowledge," - HOSEA 4:6

** You are in bondage to another man because of the debts you owe; but Jesus already paid the price for you to be free from debt! BE FREE!

Covenant Rights

God has given us a covenant right to get wealth in order for all nations of the Earth to be blessed.

It is our job to study the Word of God and put faith pressure on the promises of God until we see the manifestation in our finances.

> *"But ye are a chosen generation, a royal priesthood, an holy nation, a peculiar people; that ye should shew forth praises of Him who hath called you out of darkness into marvelous light,"* - 1 PETER 2:9

> *"And if ye be Christ's, then you are Abraham's seed, and heirs according to the promise,"* - GALATIANS 3:29

** You have a covenant right to every blessing God promised to Abraham. Be ready to give God praise through your testimony when His promises manifest in your life.

God's Promises

> *"But thou shalt remember the Lord thy God: for it is He that giveth thee power to get wealth, that He may establish His covenant which He sware unto thy fathers, as it is this day ,"*
> - DEUTERONOMY 8:18

> *"The blessing of the Lord, it maketh rich, and He addeth no sorrow with it,"* - PROVERBS 10:22

> *"Now unto Him that is able to do exceeding abundantly above all that we ask or think, according to the power that worketh in us,"*
> - EPHESIANS 3:20

"The thief cometh not, but to steal, and to kill, and to destroy: I am come that they might have life, and that they might have it more abundantly," - JOHN 10:10

** God promises to give increase, but the purpose goes beyond you and me. God's interested in fulfilling His covenant.

God's Way of Prosperity

"He that is faithful in that which is least is faithful also in much: and he that is unjust in the least is unjust also in the much,"
- LUKE 16:10

"He becometh poor that dealeth with a slack hand: but the hand of the diligent maketh rich," - PROVERBS 10:4

" For verily I say unto you, that whosoever shall say unto this mountain, Be thou removed, and be thou cast into the sea; and shall not doubt in his heart, but shall believe that those things which he saith shall come to pass; He shall have whatsoever he saith. Therefore I say unto you, what things soever ye desire, when you pray, believe that ye receive them, and ye shall have them. And when ye stand praying, forgive, if ye ought against any: that your Father also which is in heaven may forgive you your trespasses,"
- MARK 11:23-25

"But this I say, he which soweth sparingly shall reap also sparingly; and he which soweth bountifully shall reap also bountifully. Every man according as he purposeth in his heart, so let him give, not grudgingly, or of necessity: for God loveth a cheerful giver. And God is able to make all grace abound toward you; that ye, always having all sufficiency in all things, may abound to every good work," - 2 CORINTHIANS 9:6-8

"While the earth remaineth, seedtime and harvest, and cold and heat, and summer and winter, and day and night shall not cease," Genesis 8:22

"And the Lord answered me, and said, Write the vision, and make it plain upon tables, that he may run that readeth it. For the vision is yet for an appointed time, but at the end it shall speak, and not lie: though it tarry, wait for it; because it will surely come, it will not tarry," Habakkuk 2:2, 3

** God's way of prosperity involves:
1. Writing the vision and making it plain
2. Continuing to sow seed and reap a harvest
3. Being faithful with all things God has entrusted to you
4. Having faith concerning answered prayers
5. Forgiving others

WHEN IS YOUR DUE SEASON

God works based on DUE SEASON!   TAX SEASON is January 1- April 15

	GOD'S DUE SEASON	TAX SEASON
A. How do you qualify for due season? **1. You are required to do something.**	Walk not in the counsel of the ungodly, nor sit in the way of sinners, nor sit in the seat of the scornful. Delight in the law of the Lord and meditate in His law day and night. Psalm 1:1, 2	You are required to work a job in order to become eligible to receive a tax refund.
2. How long do you have to wait to see if you are due?	God says it is not for us to know the fixed or definite time or season. Be grounded in God's Word and in the process of time you will bring forth your fruit in your season. Acts 1:7, Psalms 1:3	You have to wait an entire calendar year before you find out if you are due a tax refund.
B. How will you know if you are due?	You have to apply by accepting Jesus as your Lord and Saviour and begin to do the things God requires of you.	You need to file a tax return.
C. What makes a person confident about receiving their due?	A person's level of confidence is based upon the Word of God sown in their heart.	The person's level of confidence comes from prior experience or knowledge.

WHAT IS MY PROSPERITY PLAN?

PLANNING FOR YOUR PROSPERITY

You must plan for anything you expect to achieve in life. So likewise you should also have a prosperity plan for your life. Once you understand the spiritual purpose for prosperity you must now work on the natural side. In this section, you will learn how to create a spending plan that will assist you on your way to a prosperous life.

Financial Tips of Wisdom

- ✓ Pay your tithes. It shows your commitment, obedience and faith in God.

- ✓ Plan how you will spend your income BEFORE you get your paycheck.

- ✓ Know how much money you have to spend BEFORE you go to the store.

- ✓ Get receipts and keep track of where money is spent.

- ✓ Make a list of what you need.

- ✓ Keep as little cash as possible on hand.

- ✓ Close zero balance accounts and cut up credit cards.

- ✓ Compare banks to find services to meet your needs.

- ✓ Avoid bank fees.

- ✓ Check credit report annually.

WHAT IS A SPENDING PLAN?

A spending plan is actually a budget, but I use the word spending plan because it sounds less restrictive. A spending plan is a plan on how you will spend the income that comes into your household. It is also a guideline to assist you with measuring your financial need or surplus.

Why Is a Spending Plan Important?

A spending plan is important because it allows you to plan how you will spend your income. A lot of people who spend money without a plan find themselves in debt or not having enough to pay all their monthly expenses.

How Do I Create a Spending Plan?

Each person's spending plan is unique so you will need to do several things before you can effectively create a realistic spending plan for you.

First activity: Track your daily spending habits for a week.
Second activity: Collect your monthly, quarterly, and annual expenses.

The first activity will expose where you are really spending your money. You'll be surprised at how much money you spend weekly on items like coffee, lunch, snacks, etc. You will use the Expense Tracker Worksheet to track your daily purchases. If you are not good at writing things down immediately, you can get receipts for all your purchases and write them on the Expense Tracker Worksheet at the end of each day.

The second activity will assist you with planning not only for your monthly expenses, but also for those sudden expenses which arise less often. You will write down each expense on the Monthly Spending Plan Worksheet. Start by writing down your regular monthly expense items first. You will work each of the less frequent items into your plan once you have established your monthly spending plan.

WORKSHEET LISTING

A.   Expense Tracker Worksheet
Used to track daily purchases

B.   Monthly Spending Plan Worksheet
Used to create a monthly spending plan

C.   Debt Elimination Worksheet
Used to create a debt elimination plan

D.   Account Reconcilation Worksheet
Used to balance your checkbook with the monthly bank statement

A. EXPENSE TRACKER WORKSHEET

Date	Amount	Expense	Vendor	Purpose
4/5/2011	8.49	Lunch	Longhorn Steakhouse	Lunch with co-workers
4/7/2011	4.82	Coffee	Starbuck's	Morning Coffee

MONTHLY SPENDING PLAN WORKSHEET

This section will assist you with designing a monthly spending plan for your household expenses. Let's review an example to clarify the purpose of the worksheet in detail and sample processes to use while going through your expenses.

Checklist of items you need to get started with your spending plan

✓ Completed Expense Tracker Worksheet

✓ A listing of all income you receive in your household (Pay Stubs)

✓ Utility Bills (Electric, Gas, Water, Trash, etc.)

✓ Cell Phone, Home Phone, Cable, Internet

✓ Insurance (Car, Homeowners, Renters, Life, Medical, etc.)

✓ Estimated Monthly Food Bill

✓ Credit Card Bills

✓ Child Care Expenses (Daycare, Aftercare, Summer Camp)

✓ Personal (Hair, Nails, Dry Cleaning, Laundry)

✓ Taxes (Car, House, Self-Employment)

A completed budget worksheet will identify and estimate your actual household expenses based upon how often you get paid.

B. MONTHLY SPENDING PLAN WORKSHEET

	Due Dates	Pay Day 2/4/11	Pay Day 2/18/11
Net Pay		$1,200	$1,200
Tithes		($160)	($160)
Rent	1st	($400)	($400)
Car Note	8th	($350)	
Fuel		($100)	($100)
Food		($150)	($150)
Electric	21st		($200)
Credit Card	15th	($100)	
Telephone	25th		($150)
Total Expense		($1,260)	($1,160)
Over/(Under)		($60)	$40

Definitions

Gross Pay: The amount of pay you earn before any taxes or deductions are taken out.

Net Pay: The amount of pay you receive after taxes and deductions are taken out.

Example: You get paid $1,600 every two weeks. Your taxes are $250 and you have other deductions of $150 for benefits.

Your net pay each pay period would be calculated as follows:

Every Two Weeks
```
  $1,600
- $250
- $150
= $1,200
```

Salary - Taxes - Other Deductions = Net Pay

Now you are ready to write in all your monthly household expenses. If you do not know the actual amount for an expense, estimate the amount. It is better to overestimate when going through this exercise.

The first step is to fill in your net pay for each pay date within the month. Next, list all your bills with the due date in the column next to each bill. This information will assist you in determining which bills should be paid on each pay date in order to meet your bill due date. Finally, add up all the bills to be paid with each paycheck.

In our example on page 40, it shows that we are short $60.00 on our first pay date of the month and we have a surplus of $40.00 on our second pay date of the month.

Net Pay – Expenses = Over/Under Spending

This calculation will indicate whether your household expenses are more or less than your income.

If you are over spending your money will come up short after all the bills to be paid are identified. If this occurs, take the following steps:

1. Review the worksheet and identify areas where you can make adjustments.

2. Reduce your expenses to within your spendable income.

3. Check to see if there are funds saved from any earlier pay periods. If so, you can use the funds to cover the shortage in this paycheck.

4. Review all the bills to be paid and prioritize by the following:

   ✓ Identify which bills have to be paid
   ✓ Identify which bills you can hold off until next paycheck
   ✓ Identify which bills you can pay a lower amount on
   ✓ Identify which bills you can eliminate or reduce the monthly amount of

   ** Continue to identify the above areas until you come within your budget for your paycheck.

When identifying the bills you can eliminate or reduce, think about some of the things you can function without like cable TV, Internet, premium cable channels, like HBO or Showtime, or having both a home and cell phone.

Also, if you own a home or car consider refinancing your loan to reduce your interest rate and monthly payment amount. If you have homeowners or renters insurance through a different company than your car insurance, you can usually save on insurance by using one company for both. Also, every couple of years have an insurance broker check to ensure your current insurance company is giving you the best deal.

I can recall that I had faithfully purchased my car insurance from a certain national insurance company for over 8 years. Then, I purchased a home and the mortgage broker suggested I combine my homeowners and car insurance. By making this change my six month premium for car insurance was reduced by over $200.

If you are under spending, which means you have money left from your paycheck after all bills for the month are paid, then go through the following steps below:

1. Assess monies needed for the next couple of pay period bills to determine if the extra funds are needed to cover upcoming expenses.

2. Consider areas where you can pay additional money on a debt to help accelerate the payoff process.

3. Establish a reserve or savings account to assist with unexpected expenses.

4. Consider some investment opportunities to help you save for the future.

Example

Payday	4TH	18TH
Amount available	$1,200	$1,200
Total expenses	-$1,260	- $1,160
Funds over/short	-$60	+$40

By doing this exercise in advance before you receive your paycheck you're able to see where you have a shortage on the first paycheck of the month and a surplus on the second paycheck of the month.

Several things I want you to take note of in this example.

The rent expense is $800; which is a large expense. By planning how you spend your income in advance, you can save $400 from each paycheck so you still have funds to pay other expenses.

1. There is a $60 shortage on the first paycheck, which can be reduced by $40 by simply adjusting the amount saved for rent on the first paycheck. If I save $360 on the first paycheck and $440 on the second paycheck, I will have saved the $800 for rent by the end of the month and only have a $20 shortage.

2. Then I can reduce my funds for food to $140 per paycheck and now I am balanced for the month.

See budget sheet on page 40.

DEBT ELIMINATION WORKSHEET

This worksheet should be used to list all your credit cards, student loans, house notes, car notes, or any expenses with a monthly balance until paid off.

Fill out the worksheet with the information requested for all debts indicated above.

This worksheet will allow you to do two important things:

A. Determine how much debt you owe your creditors
B. Develop a strategy on how to reduce and eliminate this debt

Determining the Amount of Debt Owed Your Creditors

This is an important step which requires you to sit down and organize the information needed to fill out this sheet. You may have to call creditors and pull out your monthly billing statements to get the information for each bill.

> **** If you are believing GOD to cancel your debt, you need to know exactly what you owe and to whom. GOD could put the money in your hands today and because you are unaware of what you owe you will spend the money and miss your opportunity to cancel your debt. ****

Developing a Strategy to Reduce Debt

There are several strategies which can be used by an individual to devise a plan of attack to reduce your debt to zero.

A. Interest Strategy

Compare the interest rates you are paying on the various debts. In most cases, you want to focus on paying off the high-interest debts first.

Exception: When you can completely pay off a smaller debt amount. This will reduce your monthly pay out because the monthly amount for that debt will be eliminated.

Example: You have $800 extra dollars

Debt	Balance	Monthly	Interest Rate
Visa	$600	$60	12.5%
Student Loan	$3,000	$100	8.0%
MasterCard	$1,500	$501	16.9%

Normally with the interest rate strategy you would pay off the MasterCard account first because it has the highest interest rate. You would pay the minimum on all other debts and put any extra funds toward the MasterCard account until paid off.

In this example, if you had a lump sum or extra $800, you would pay off the Visa account and pay the extra $200 toward the MasterCard Account. After you pay off the Visa, you free up an extra $60 a month because the Visa account would be paid in full.

B. Smaller Debt Strategy

Pay off the smaller debts amounts first. This will reduce your monthly pay out once you completely pay a debt off. You should still pay attention to interest rates because the longer it takes you to pay these debts off the more you pay in interest.

Questions:

Should I do a debt consolidation loan?

Here are some things to consider:
1. Only include debt with a higher interest rate than the interest rate of the debt consolidation loan.

2. Compare what your monthly payment would be versus what you are currently paying.

3. Make sure you have an overall savings with the new loan.

Should I do a homeowner's line of credit?

Here are some things to consider:
1. Remember, you're backing the loan with your house. This means if you cannot pay the creditor, they can put a lien on your house.

   A lien means before you can sell the house the lien amount must be satisfied.

2. The tax write-off of the interest paid is why a homeowner's line of credit is so popular.

   Caution: This interest is only deductible on your taxes up to the equity in your house.

Example:
Value of House – Principal Amount Still Owed = Equity in House

House Value	$80,000
Principal Amount Owed	$78,000
Equity in House	$2,000

Only $2,000 of the interest paid would be deductible.

TIP:
By paying extra on your house/car notes you can save dollars on interest and accelerate your payoff time period.

C. DEBT ELIMINATION WORKSHEET

Creditors: Name/ Address/Phone	Account Number(s)	Current Balance(s)	Monthly Payment(s)	Months Remaining(s)	Interest Rate(s)

ACCOUNT RECONCILIATION WORKSHEET

This worksheet is used to balance your checkbook with your bank statement. It is important to do this on a monthly basis. The bank can make a mistake or you could forget to include a transaction in your checkbook register. This process will allow you to locate any missing transactions.

Outstanding Items - a check/deposit is considered outstanding when it is recorded in your checkbook, but has not yet appeared on your bank statement.

1. Begin by putting the ending balance shown on your bank statement at the top of the worksheet.
2. Next, review all transactions posted on the bank statement and compare it to the transactions listed in your check register.
3. Third, identify and list any outstanding checks and deposits not posted on the bank statement but that are listed on your check register.
4. Fourth, identify any missing items or bank service charges/interest not listed in your check register but that are posted on the bank statement.
5. Finally, the adjusted bank statement balance should equal your check register balance.

**** If there are any differences you need to complete the above process again to identify the difference in the bank statement and your check register.

TIPS:
Always check your addition and subtraction on your check register to ensure accuracy.

Make checkmarks next to each transaction identified on both the bank statement and your check register.

D. ACCOUNT RECONCILIATION WORKSHEET

Ending Balance on Bank Statement $_____

Add: Outstanding Deposits

$_____
$_____
$_____
$_____
$_____

Total Outstanding Deposits $_____

Minus: Outstanding Checks

$_____
$_____
$_____
$_____
$_____

Total Outstanding Checks $_____

Adjusted Bank Statement Balance $_____

Checkbook Ending Balance $_____

Minus: Bank Charges $_____

Add: Interest Received $_____

Adjusted Checkbook Balance $_____

Balance Differences $_____

MONEY DOES MATTER

SECTION III

HOW CAN I PROTECT MY PROSPERITY?

PROTECTING YOUR PROSPERITY

One way to protect your prosperity is to plan for unexpected expenses. This can be done by setting aside a financial reserve of at least three months of your salary for unexpected expenses like medical bills, car repairs, home repairs, etc. Another way to protect your wealth if you can't set aside three months reserve is to get insurance to assist you with unexpected expenses.

INSURANCE

Insurance is a <u>risk management</u> technique primarily used to guard against the <u>risk</u> of a contingent, <u>uncertain</u> loss that may be suffered by individuals or entities that transfers the liability of this loss from one interested person or entity to another.

Types of Insurance

Homeowner's Insurance – This insurance is used to provide for the expense of rebuilding your home if it is damaged and replace your furnishings if destroyed. It's important to keep a listing of your personal belongings with estimated values and pictures in a fireproof safe.

Renter's Insurance – If you rent an apartment then renter's insurance will provide you with funds to replace your personal belonging if the apartment building is destroyed or your personal belongings are damaged. You should keep a listing of your personal belongings and pictures in a fireproof safe.

Short Term Disability Insurance – This insurance provides you a percentage of your pay if you are unable to work due to illness or medical conditions. The timeframe you can receive the insurance is usually up to 13 weeks after missing one week of work.

Long Term Disability Insurance – This insurance provides you a percentage of your pay if you're unable to work due to illness or medical conditions in excess of 14 weeks.

Life Insurance – This insurance covers you when your life ends on Earth. It leaves money for your beneficiary (whoever you designate) to pay for your funeral costs as well as any unpaid bills you still owe at your time of death.

Two common types of life insurance are term life and whole life.

Term life is a life insurance policy that ends after a specific term and pays out at your death a designated amount which you select.

Whole life is a life insurance policy that is meant to last over your whole life which is usually a longer period of time than a term life policy. The premium is higher on a whole life policy because the premium will not increase over your life. A term life policy premium may increase at the end of the term when it is time to renew the policy.

Whole life policies carry a cash value which increases over time and can be borrowed against in time of need. Upon death, any outstanding loans will be paid off before the death benefit amount is paid out.

This is important insurance to have on yourself as well as your children and elderly parents. There are many cases where children pass and the parents do not have any money to bury their child. Also, when adults pass who do not have insurance your loved ones are forced to figure out how to pay for your funeral expenses.

Scenario A

Jan recently had some medical work completed which is requiring her to be out of work for six weeks. Short-term disability only pays 60 percent of her salary.

What can Jan do to ensure she can meet her financial obligations for the next six weeks?

1. Create a list of everything she needs to spend for the next six weeks.

2. Create a budget based upon the expected income in the next six weeks to see where there may be a surplus or shortage.

3. See what funds may be available in a savings account and other insurance she may have.

4. Call creditors and let them know her situation. If she's been making payments on time, they may be willing to allow her to skip a payment or reduce payment amounts or interest rates.

Doing this exercise in advance will help you make the necessary adjustments on paper before you get and spend the income. Assess your needs first!

Scenario B

Bob and Mary's home is in the process of going into foreclosure.

What are some steps they can take now?

1. Examine their situation to understand what caused them to get behind on their payments.

2. Determine how long do they expect their current financial situation to last? (Unknown, short term or long term)

3. Call their mortgage company and explain the situation.

4. Put their house on the market.

5. Check with approved HUD agencies which offer special programs for homeowners in financial distress.

CREDIT

What is credit?

Credit is a history of how you pay your bills.

Your credit represents "You."

Here are a few definitions from the dictionary:

1. The quality of being credible or trustworthy
2. The favorable estimate of a person's character; reputation; good name
3. Trust in one's integrity in money matters and one's ability to meet payments when due

Credit is used in the world's system to decide if a person/entity will obtain funds requested. The lender/creditor uses your credit score as one of the factors to determine if they're willing to lend you funds. The lower your credit score, the higher interest you will be asked to pay if approved. This means people with good credit can obtain a loan at a lower interest rate than someone with bad credit. Depending on how low your credit score is, you may even be denied credit.

Here are a few things you can do to improve your credit:

✓ Pay your bills on time

✓ Check your credit report at all three bureaus

✓ Know your rights as a consumer

Credit Management

Nationwide Consumer Reporting Agencies collect and maintain a history of your credit activity as reported by lenders and creditors with whom you have accounts. They also collect public record information such as bankruptcies, civil judgments, tax liens and collection items.

The three main consumer reporting agencies are:
- Equifax
- TransUnion
- Experian

1. **www.annualcreditreport.com**
   Website for obtaining a free credit report annually from each of the three consumer reporting agencies.

2. **www.ftc.gov**
   Website for the Federal Trade Commission (FTC). Their purpose is to protect the American consumer. You can obtain information about debt collections, do-not-call registries, consumer complaints, identity theft and other information.

3. **http://www.ftc.gov/bcp/edu/pubs/consumer/credit/cre03.shtm**
   Contains a manual on the FTC website for building a better credit report.

4. **www.justice.gov/ust**
   Website for the United States Department of Justice where you can get a list of approved credit counselors by state.

CERTIFICATE OF COMPLETION

YOU HAVE JUST COMPLETED THE SPENDING PLAN WORKSHEETS!
You are on your way to debt-freedom. Remember, you must continue to do the spiritual things as well as the natural things. God has put funds in your hands to see how you will manage them.

You must be faithful over what God has entrusted to you in order to receive more. Begin to write down what you will do with the surplus funds. God is waiting on you to get organized and committed to doing whatever it takes for Him to release all your debts.

1. First, begin by writing everything down and making it plain. When others see it, they can agree and run with the vision (Habakkuk 2:2).

2. Next, find scriptures that show examples of what you believe God will do in your life. Confess these scriptures out of your mouth as many times as possible (Ezra 10:11). Put God in remembrance of His Word knowing that He will bring what you confess to pass (2 Timothy 1:6).

3. Finally, continue to build yourself up in faith no matter what comes your way. God is able to do exceedingly, abundantly, above what you can ask or think. Continue proclaiming, even when the situation looks, feels or sounds bad. We operate by the Word of God, and we have what we say according to God's Word.

Be encouraged in the Lord and press toward the high mark set before you. Consistency and obedience are the keys which will lead you not only to financial prosperity, but to complete life prosperity—prosperity in every area of your life.

Remember, no man will make you rich, but God only.

_____   _____
Signature   Date

BLANK
FORMS

A. EXPENSE TRACKER WORKSHEET

Date	Amount	Expense	Vendor	Purpose

B. MONTHLY SPENDING PLAN WORKSHEET

	Due Dates	1st Pay Day	2nd Pay Day
Monthly Bills			
Total Expense			
Over (Under)			

C. DEBT ELIMINATION WORKSHEET

Creditors: Name/ Address/Phone	Account Number(s)	Current Balance(s)	Monthly Payment(s)	Months Remaining(s)	Interest Rate(s)

D. ACCOUNT RECONCILIATION WORKSHEET

Ending Balance on Bank Statement $_____

Add: Outstanding Deposits

$_____
$_____
$_____
$_____
$_____

Total Outstanding Deposits $_____

Minus: Outstanding Checks

$_____
$_____
$_____
$_____
$_____

Total Outstanding Checks $_____

Adjusted Bank Statement Balance $_____

Checkbook Ending Balance $_____

Minus: Bank Charges $_____

Add: Interest Received $_____

Adjusted Checkbook Balance $_____

Balance Differences $_____

MONEY DOES MATTER